TAK

TAKING THE ICE

THE MIGHTY DUCKS OF ANAHEIM

Dean Chadwin

POLESTAR
BOOK PUBLISHERS

TAKING THE ICE

Copyright © 1994 by Dean Chadwin
No part of this publication may be reproduced, stored in a retrieval system or transmitted, in any form or by any means, without prior permission of the publisher or, in case of photocopying or other reprographic copying, a licence from CANCOPY (Canadian Reprography Collective), 214 King Street West, Toronto, Ontario, M5H 3S6.

Published by:
Polestar Press Ltd.
1011 Commercial Drive, Second Floor
Vancouver, BC
Canada V5L 3X1

Cover design by Jim Brennan.
Editing by Julian Ross.
Cover and author photographs by Chris Relke.
Interior photos by Chris Relke, Ted Soqui and Frank Prado.
Printed in Canada by Best Book Manufacturers.

Canadian Cataloguing in Publication Data

Chadwin, Dean, 1965-
    Taking the ice

ISBN 0-919591-33-7
    1. Mighty Ducks of Anaheim (Hockey Team)—History. I. Title.
GV848.M53C52 1994   j796.962'64'0979496   C94-910612-7

TAKING THE ICE
THE MIGHTY DUCKS OF ANAHEIM

TAKING THE ICE ● 7

PIECES OF THE PUZZLE ● 16

BIG KIDS ● 24

THE WAY IT IS ● 32

THE UNITED NATIONS ● 39

THE NEW GUYS ● 45

MIGHTY STATS ● 55

To Adrienne Lee Chadwin, who read to me when I was a child and suggested that I write this book for other little ones.

1

TAKING THE ICE

The Mighty Ducks of Anaheim—one of the newest teams in the National Hockey League—is among the most popular teams in all of professional sports. But before the team ever took the ice, a number of tasks had to be completed. Everything started in Anaheim, California.

Anaheim is a large city in Southern California, about thirty miles south of downtown Los Angeles. It's home to Disneyland, and the famous Knott's Berry Farm is just a few miles away. A few years ago, the city council of Anaheim decided to build a new indoor arena for concerts and sporting events. The arena was very expensive (over $100 million) and the city needed to find a sports team to play there.

Before the team even took the ice, the Mighty Ducks's logo was loved by young fans all across North America.

The arena was almost finished, and still no basketball or hockey team had decided to move in. People in Anaheim—especially those on city council—were worried. In Los Angeles, however, was a man with a plan. Los Angeles already had a hockey team, the Kings. The Kings featured Wayne Gretzky, hockey's greatest player, and were owned by Bruce McNall, the man with the plan.

McNall wanted another hockey team to be based in Southern California. He asked his friend Michael Eisner, the President of the Disney company, if Disney would like to own an NHL team. At first, Eisner wasn't interested. Even though Disney has made two very successful movies about a youth hockey team, they had never owned a sports team before. McNall kept asking Eisner, and Mike, whose own kids loved to play hockey, grew curious. In December, 1992, Eisner decided it was time for Disney to join the NHL. He would put the team in the new Anaheim Arena. The people of Anaheim breathed a huge sigh of relief.

So now the rink had a home team and an owner, but no team name, no players and no manager. Eisner decided to tie his new team to his movie team and call it the Mighty Ducks of Anaheim. Because they were Ducks, Eisner named the Anaheim Arena "The Pond". When he announced the team's new name in March of 1993, people made jokes.

Michael Eisner didn't worry about what other people thought. He hired an experienced team president, Tony Tavares, to assemble a group of people that would find the best players available. Tavares had worked in arena management for years and knew a lot about hockey. He would have to be smart and fast. The Mighty Ducks had to be ready to play in the NHL in just seven months.

What Tavares had to do was put together a front office staff. He needed people who knew how to sell tickets, how to advertise the team and how to produce broadcasts. Tavares knew about hockey, but it wasn't his life. He needed to find a general manager whose life had been devoted to hockey.

Jack Ferreira's life was hockey. He'd played the game as a young boy. He became good enough to be an All-American goalie in college for Boston University in the late '60s. After his playing career ended, Ferreira became an assistant coach. He then took a scouting job with the Hartford Whalers. He later scouted for the Calgary Flames and the New York Rangers before eventually becoming a general manager for the Minnesota North Stars and then the San Jose Sharks.

Tavares decided to hire Ferreira as general manager for two reasons. He had already been through an expansion in San Jose and the team he'd helped put together in Calgary had won a Stanley Cup.

"Jack's experiences in Calgary and the fact that he'd been through an expansion in San Jose were important," says Tavares. "We hired Jack because he knew his way around the NHL."

The team needed an assistant general manager to handle the amateur and pro scouting. Tavares wanted Jack to talk to Pierre Gauthier, who was the scouting director for the Quebec Nordiques. "I suggested to Jack that we had to organize things fast. I asked him if he knew Pierre Gauthier. I was candid with him and told him that Pierre finished second to him in the sweepstakes to be GM. Jack graciously agreed to interview him, and he ended up hiring him."

The hirings of Ferreira and Gauthier were announced in late March. The player draft was just three months away. The two old friends were a perfect fit. "Jack had been scouting the pros, and Pierre had been concentrating on the juniors," said Tavares. "That made us feel very comfortable that we were going into the draft prepared. We had to fit our needs because of the emergency nature of the situation."

Ferreira and Gauthier hired scouts to look for new players. The new players would need team colors to wear. In early June, Eisner showed off the Mighty Duck uniform. "The official logo, as you can see, is a mean goalie mask," Eisner announced.

● 12   **TAKING THE ICE**

TED SOQUI

The city of Anaheim built a big new arena that looked more like a shopping mall than a rink. At first, nobody wanted to play there. When the Ducks finally decided to play in Anaheim, they named the new building the Pond.

THE MIGHTY DUCKS OF ANAHEIM

"We wanted something that was between Disneyesque and hockey-mean. Now all we need is a coach and players and we'll be in great shape."

The new logo was a hit right away. Adults and kids everywhere bought jerseys and caps. It was the Mighty Ducks' first success. The next step would be to get players who could make them a success on ice.

The Mighty Ducks would get their first players from the other teams already in the league. The 1993 draft was held in Quebec City. In the expansion draft, new teams choose players which other teams have pre-selected to be unprotected, or eligible for draft. Anaheim and the Florida Panthers were the two new teams participating in the expansion draft. The first player the Mighty Ducks chose was Guy Hebert, a goalie from the St. Louis Blues. The first defenseman they chose was Alexei Kasatonov, who had played for the New Jersey Devils. Alexei had been a star in the Soviet Union for many years, winning Olympic and world titles. The first forward they picked was Steven King of the New York Rangers. In total, the Mighty Ducks selected twenty-four players from other teams.

None of the players were stars, although many of them had played in the NHL for a number of years. The other teams kept their best players, of course, but the Ducks believed they'd gotten some good players. Maybe they'd become even better if they had a chance to play more often. They might not be superstars, but Ferreira was happy because he had big players with a lot of experience.

In the amateur draft, the Ducks would have the chance to pick future stars. They took Paul Kariya with their first pick. Kariya was already more famous than any of the older players the Ducks had already taken. Kariya was a small forward (5' 10", 175 pounds) who could skate very fast and make perfect passes. As a boy growing up in Vancouver, he'd been a fan of Wayne Gretzky. He wore his uniform like the Great One and even tried to imitate his moves.

Some people called Kariya "The Next One" to show he would follow in Gretzky's footsteps. Paul showed everyone how good he could be when he led the University of Maine to an NCAA title in his first year. He became the first freshman ever to win the Hobey Baker Award for best college player in the United States. Kariya could have played for the Ducks right away, but instead he decided to play for the Canadian Olympic team.

Kariya wasn't the only player the Ducks got in the amateur draft. They also took three skilled Russians: a defenseman, a forward, and a goalie. Nikolai Tsulygin, a 6' 3" defenseman, was already bigger than most other players though he'd just turned eighteen. He wasn't quite ready for the NHL yet. Valeri Karpov, the forward, was a good passer like Kariya. He would play against Paul in the Olympics for the Russian team. The goalie, Mikhail Shtalenkov, was older than the other players and had already spent a year in the United States. He might be ready to help the Ducks soon.

Now the players needed a coach. Ferreira interviewed Ron Wilson, who had worked as an assistant coach in Vancouver. Ron had been a defenseman in the NHL. He'd also played for teams in Europe. His father and his uncle had both coached in the NHL. Ron wanted to coach a new team, too.

Ferreira liked Wilson and asked Tavares to interview him. "The thing that impressed me most was what a heady coach he was," said Tavares. "Ron just impressed me with his knowledge of players in the league, his preparation for a game, how he analyzed teams, how he analyzed strengths and weaknesses, and how he designed a game plan to exploit those strengths and weaknesses."

Wilson was the perfect coach for a new team. The Mighty Ducks now had everything in place: a rink, a logo, ticket-sellers, scouts, coaches, broadcasters, and players. After months of hard work, they were ready to take the ice.

2

PIECES OF THE PUZZLE

The Mighty Ducks started their first season with five games at the Pond. They lost the first game, against Detroit, by five goals. Nothing went right. In the second game, against the New York Islanders, the Ducks played better. They made it into overtime, but they lost again. The fans wondered when the Mighty Ducks first win would come.

The team had come close. The players and the coaches believed they could do it. Terry Yake, one of the team's best scorers, summed up everyone's feelings. "We've made a big step forward," said Yake, "and our games are going to continue to improve."

In their next game, the Ducks would meet the Edmonton Oilers at the Pond. The Mighty Ducks

THE MIGHTY DUCKS OF ANAHEIM 17

Wild Wing, the Mighty Ducks' official mascot, fired up the fans before each game at the Pond.

TED SOQUI

wanted to become as good as the Oilers had been. As a team, the Oilers won five Stanley Cups in the 1980s featuring an all-star roster of players that included Wayne Gretzky, Mark Messier, Paul Coffey and Grant Fuhr. The Ducks would have had a tough time trying to beat that team. They were lucky that none of those players were with the Oilers anymore. The Oilers were rebuilding. The Ducks had a good chance of winning if they played well.

During the second loss, the offense was good some of the time. The defense was good most of the time. It wasn't enough. For a new team to win, everyone has to contribute. What the Mighty Ducks needed was to put all the pieces of the puzzle together.

The first piece of the puzzle was a little revenge. Three Mighty Ducks had played for the Oilers. They were centers Shaun Van Allen and Anatoli Semenov and goalie Ron Tugnutt. The Oilers had traded Semenov to Vancouver. Before the expansion draft, the Oilers failed to protect Tugnutt and Van Allen. The Mighty Ducks snatched them up. All three skaters wanted to win to prove their old team wrong. They would play harder than ever. Ron Wilson, Tugnutt's coach, knew how his goalie felt and named him the starter.

The second piece of the puzzle was a plan. The coaches had to tell the players how they wanted them to play. In the first two games, the Mighty Ducks had started slow. Wilson wanted his players to come out fast against the Oilers. They should be excited, but not nervous. He hoped they wouldn't make any bad mistakes. Let the *Oilers* get in trouble, he told them.

The third piece of the puzzle was the fans. Even though the Ducks hadn't won a regular season game yet, the fans kept coming to the Pond. They wanted to see their team win. Before the game, the team's mascot fired up the fans. Wild Wing, a huge duck with a goalie mask and skates, descended from the roof of the Pond as the crowd cheered. When Wild Wing hit the ice, he danced to rock-and-roll songs. Duck supporters, especially young ones, got even more excited. Right away, Wild Wing was the most popular Duck. He still receives more mail than any of the players. When the players took the ice, it was clear Wild Wing had done his job. The crowd erupted with applause for their Mighty Ducks of Anaheim.

Wilson had asked for a quick start and hoped for Oiler mistakes. During the game's first shift, Joe Sacco, the fastest Duck, made a strong move toward the Edmonton net. One of the Oiler defensemen panicked and pulled Joe down. The referee raised his arm and blasted his whistle. Penalty, Oilers.

The Mighty Ducks had a power play. Sean Hill,

Former Edmonton Oiler Shaun Van Allen showed up his old team during the Ducks' first win.

a young defenseman who had scored the Ducks' first goal, fired the puck at Bill Ranford, the Oiler goalie. The rebound squirted free. Troy Loney, the Mighty Duck captain, grabbed the puck and slipped it by Ranford. The game had just started and the scoreboard read: MIGHTY DUCKS 1   OILERS 0.

Things went from bad to worse for the Oilers as the Ducks were able to put two more shots past Ranford. Between periods, the Oiler coach decided to change goalies, replacing Ranford with Fred Brathwaite. He hoped the Oilers would start to play better. Even a new goalie didn't slow down the Ducks. The Ducks continued to fire pucks at the net. Finally, Terry Yake made a beautiful play. He faked a shot. The Oiler defenseman made a mistake and went down to block the shot. Terry skated around the defenseman on the ice and passed the puck to Bill Houlder. Bill had rushed to the open area. He caught the puck and beat the new Oiler goalie. Now it was MIGHTY DUCKS 4   OILERS 0.

It looked like the Ducks were going to win their first game. The offense had done their job. The team had a big lead. Now it was up to the defense and the goalie. Two minutes after Houlder scored, the Oilers scored a power-play goal. The Oilers started skating harder, outplaying the Ducks for the rest of the period. Neither team scored. Twenty minutes left and the Ducks still had a three-goal lead.

The Oilers refused to quit. They scored again less than two minutes into the third period. Now the Ducks were getting a little nervous. Could they hang on?

Five minutes later, the situation grew worse. An Oiler stood in front of the Ducks net to distract Tugnutt. Mighty Duck defenseman Alexei Kasatonov hit the Oiler with a stick on the chest to clear him out of the slot. The referee saw the whole play. He penalized Kasatonov with a five-minute major for high-sticking and a game misconduct.

Now the Ducks were without their top defenseman while trying to protect the lead. Even worse, the major penalty meant the next five minutes would be spent a man short no matter how many times Edmonton scored. A minute and a half into the power play, the Oilers scored again. The four goal lead was now one. Eleven minutes remained in the game. The crowd grew nervous and quiet.

The Ducks' penalty-killers knew they had to come through. They stayed together to block dangerous passes. They allowed only long or bad-angle shots. Tugnutt made the tough saves. The Mighty Ducks survived the rest of the power play without allowing a goal.

Now the Ducks only wanted the clock to run out. They played dump-and-chase hockey, firing the puck deep into the Oiler zone whenever they got the chance. The Ducks took just four shots on goal for the whole period. The strategy worked and the Oilers' chances dwindled as well.

With a little more than a minute to go, Edmonton pulled their goaltender in favor of an extra forward. The Ducks continued to clear their own zone. Tugnutt made one more great save. More than fifteen thousand fans, young and old, rose from their seats and urged their team on. Screaming as loud as they could, they counted down the game's final seconds.

10...9...8...7...6...5. The Oilers made one last rush. 4...3...2. They tried a centering pass. Joe Sacco stole it and shot the puck down the ice. 1. The Mighty Ducks of Anaheim had won their first game. The scoreboard confirmed it: MIGHTY DUCKS 4 OILERS 3.

The crowd roared with joy. Fireworks exploded around the scoreboard. Wilson screamed "yes!" to assistant coach Al Sims and broke into a huge smile on the bench. Then the bench emptied. All the Mighty Ducks jumped on their goalie Ron Tugnutt. He'd gained his revenge on his old team. He was named the number one star of the game.

Wilson smiled as he talked to the press. "You know, our team's not used to a lead like that," Wilson said. "But don't talk to me. Go talk to the players. They won it."

In the locker room, Tugnutt was smiling, too. "We had a solid first period, then we sat back a little. We let them get back in. They got hungry, and we got nervous," Tugnutt said before describing his final save. "It was just a reaction. It was a prayer. I had to get up and get over to block it."

All the players talked about developing a killer instinct. They wanted to keep teams down once they got a lead. As they talked, they were thinking about the good feelings that would linger. The heat was off. They were winners tonight. For the first time, they had put together all the pieces of the puzzle.

3

BIG KIDS

The life of a pro hockey player seems really exciting. They get to travel, play in front of big crowds, and try to win the Stanley Cup. The truth is the Mighty Ducks aren't that different from you. Even though they get paid very well for playing hockey, they're still just big kids.

Most hockey players have one thing in common: they started playing hockey when they were really young. Many players learned how to skate almost at the same time as they learned how to walk. It helps to get an early start.

Mighty Duck goalie Guy Hebert started early. His older brother played hockey all the time and Guy liked to tag along. None of his brother's friends liked to stop the puck so they made little Guy the

Big kid Bobby Dollas had his best season because he enjoyed playing for Coach Wilson.

goalie. Guy wanted to dive around after pucks more than he wanted to skate up and down the ice. He kept doing what he liked to do: stopping pucks.

If you watch Guy practice today, he doesn't skate that fast. Of course, goalies do wear heavy equipment, but he's not the best skater. He is one of the best puck stoppers because that's what he practiced when he was a boy. The best part is he didn't even know he was practicing, he was just having fun doing what he liked to do.

The things you love to do now will probably be the things you'll like doing when you're a grown-up. If you love to read, you'll probably keep reading the rest of your life. If you love hockey now, you'll probably keep playing even if you don't make it all the way to the pros. Most of the Ducks would play hockey for fun even if they had different jobs.

Mighty Duck practices can be hard-working and serious. But when the work is over, the players and the coaches often stay on the ice playing pick-up games. They laugh, they try new moves, they show off. They can't stop playing games. When they come off the ice, they play ping-pong in the locker room. When they go home, a lot of the players play video games or play with their kids. They love to play. After all, they're just big kids.

Long before they got to the NHL, many of the Ducks had jobs when they were teenagers. They worked delivering papers or bagging groceries so they could buy a new pair of skates or extra sticks. They had jobs and played for their high school or junior teams, but they still got their schoolwork done. They would work hard so they could play later.

Just like you do now, they had their favorite players when they were growing up. For many of the Ducks, their idol was Wayne Gretzky. When they were kids, they just hoped they could just meet him someday. Now they get to play against him.

They remember what it's like to be a young fan. When the Ducks played a game against the Canucks in Vancouver, it was a chance for Garry Valk to play his former teammates. He also would play before his old fans. During the final warm-ups, a five-year-old boy in a Ducks' sweater pressed his face against the glass. He watched Garry closely. During his last lap around the ice, Valk charged right up to the boards. He stopped and flipped a puck over the boards to the young fan. Mighty Ducks never forget what it's like to be a kid.

Whatever you do, you shouldn't give up when things are tough. Ask Todd Ewen. He played all the time when he was young. When he became a teenager, his coaches put him on the ice less and less. He was getting frustrated. Even his mom thought that maybe Todd should quit. Todd loved to play and he kept going to practices and games. Suddenly, he got bigger and stronger and faster, and became more coordinated. He started to play more, finally making it all the way to the big leagues.

Todd didn't know he was going to make it. He just knew he liked hockey so he kept playing. Even if you're not the best, if you're having fun, that's good enough.

Todd is an enforcer. His job is to protect his teammates. One time Todd took the shirt right off his opponent's back and danced around the ice showing the jersey to all his teammates. The man with no shirt was bent over. He wasn't crying. He was laughing.

The jersey in Todd's hand belonged to his coach, Ron Wilson. They'd been playing together after practice. Ron likes to play, too. He plays in pick-up games and ping-pong games. Knowing that their coach likes to play helps keep the Ducks relaxed. Ron doesn't even believe in long practices to punish the team for bad games. He knows that the Ducks understand they have to work hard. He respects his players enough to trust them.

Because of Ron's approach, the Mighty Ducks had a great first year on the ice. Fifteen players set personal records for points scored. Players who had been fourth-liners or minor-leaguers reached new heights. The Ducks won 33 out of 84 games, tying the Florida Panthers for the expansion record. They even set a new record for a first year team by winning 19 road games. On one road trip to western Canada they beat the Vancouver Canucks, Edmonton Oilers, Calgary Flames and Winnipeg Jets.

Defenseman Bobby Dollas—a five-year veteran in the league—had his first good NHL season and credited Wilson. "I've been on some teams where you dread coming to the rink," said Dollas, who played for a half-dozen coaches on three other NHL teams. "I've always had a problem playing for coaches that rant and rave. You don't feel comfortable. You're always on edge. In this dressing room, everybody gets along real well. A lot of guys here are happy."

Happy players are just like big kids. They play hard during the game, but they goof around with each other when they're together in locker rooms, or travelling on buses or planes. After a win on the road in Edmonton, Wilson was really late catching the bus. There was a good reason. The team had suffered a few injuries, and Ron had called back to Anaheim to get new players sent on the road.

The players were bored. They had a game the next day in Vancouver. They wanted to get there as soon as possible so they could go to sleep. They begged the driver to leave Ron behind. He refused. Then they asked him to at least beep the horn. The

Guy Hebert, seen here making a big save, learned how to dive for pucks when he was a little kid.

driver wouldn't do it. When Ron finally got near the bus after everyone had been waiting fifteen minutes, Stu Grimson ran up the aisle and slammed the horn four times: Beep! Beep! Beep! Beep! Ron nearly jumped out of his pants. Everybody on the bus had a big laugh.

Even big kids know life's more than just games and jokes. The Ducks know they can do a lot to help the other people in their community. When bad fires hit Southern California in the fall of 1993, the Ducks wanted to lend a hand. They put together a charity exhibition game with the Kings. The game was called Ice the Fire.

Ice the Fire was played at the Pond in early December. The Ducks and Kings played for fun and they invited celebrities to join them. There were TV and movie stars on the ice, even the Hanson Brothers from the movie *Slapshot*. The two teams played for fun, trying moves they'd never try in a real game. Goalies carried the puck and tried to score.

Three players made the game even more special: Cammi Granato, Erin Whitten and Manon Rheaume joined the other players on the ice. Cammi's brother Tony plays forward for the Kings, while Cammi plays forward for the U.S. national women's team, one of the best in the world.

Erin and Manon play goalie for the world-champion Canadian team. Manon has played in an exhibition game for the NHL's Tampa Bay Lightning. Both Erin and Manon play in the minor professional leagues when they're not playing for Canada. By the time you're old enough to play in the NHL, women will probably be in the league. If you're a girl who thinks she doesn't have a chance to make a career out of playing hockey, don't give up. You could be a star like Cammi, Erin, and Manon.

All the stars raised hundreds of thousands of dollars for charity. It was a good night for big kids with big hearts. The players and fans alike had fun. The next time someone asks you why you like hockey, you know what to tell them. Because it's fun. If they don't believe you, tell them to ask one of the big kids.

4

THE WAY IT IS

Hockey is a game of stops and starts. You never know what's going to happen next. That uncertainty makes the game exciting and challenging. It's important for a young player to learn how to be ready for anything. That's the way it is.

During the season, pro hockey players have one thing on their mind: the next game. Bob Corkum was one of the best Mighty Ducks during their first year. He scored 23 goals, won most face-offs, and slowed down the opponent's first-line center. Bob tried to prepare the same way for every game.

When the Mighty Ducks have a game at night, they hold a pre-game skate early in the morning. Bob gets up before practice and goes to a restaurant to have breakfast. After his meal, he skates as hard

THE MIGHTY DUCKS OF ANAHEIM 35

Bobby Corkum played well every night for the Mighty Ducks because he always prepared himself for the game.

as he can during practice.

If he's in Anaheim, Bob goes home after practice and plays with his two young kids. In the afternoon when he gets tired, he takes a nap. When he wakes up, he has a pre-game meal with lots of carbohydrates. Carbohydrates are in foods like spaghetti, bread, and potatoes. They give him the energy he needs for the night's game.

Bob gets to the rink a few hours before the game and checks his equipment. He gets dressed in his practice clothes. Then he joins his teammates for the pre-game meeting. Ron Wilson and the other coaches tell the players about their opponents. They also talk to them about the Mighty Ducks' strategy for the game.

After the meeting, Bob takes the ice with the other Ducks in a pre-game skate. He zooms around the ice, trying to get loose and ready for the game. After the skate, the players wait in the locker room for the game to start. Bob might talk to a teammate about an opponent or watch a video tape of a prior game. He might just listen to loud music to get psyched up. Whatever it takes, when the puck is dropped, he's ready to go.

Bob had a great year because he was ready every night. Late in the year, however, Bob got an unlucky break. In a game in Philadelphia against the Flyers, Bob got hurt. One of the Flyers accidentally let his skate hit the front of Bob's boot. Even when he was a kid, Bob wore his boot flap down. He still does. What would have been little more than a scratch became a serious injury because the flap was down. The skate sliced the tendon on the front of his right ankle. Bob had to spend the off-season doing exercises to get his ankle back in shape.

Not every game day turned out exactly the same. In February, the Mighty Ducks had a game against the Vancouver Canucks. Head coach Ron Wilson had been a coach with Vancouver the year before. When he was named coach of the Mighty Ducks, he put Mighty Duck bumper stickers up in the Vancouver offices.

The Vancouver coaches decided to get him back. While the Ducks were practicing, the coaches put Canuck bumper stickers all over Ron's car. When Ron went to his car after practice, he couldn't believe it. It took him half an hour to get them all off his car. He was angry, but he got the last laugh later that night. The Mighty Ducks shut out the high-scoring Canucks.

Wilson was exceptionally happy. "It's very special to beat my old team," Wilson told reporters, "especially since their staff bumper-stickered my new car today. Payback is sweet."

Another thing that's sweet is a player's first NHL goal. It's especially sweet if the player thought

Don McSween played many seasons in the minors; he scored his first NHL goal as a Mighty Duck.

he'd never make it to the NHL. Don McSween's chances were so slim that the Mighty Ducks didn't even invite him to their first training camp. When they suffered a number of injuries to their defensemen, they called up Don from their farm club in San Diego. He fit in right away, impressing his coach and teammates. He even got a chance to play before his friends and relatives back home in Detroit. He made two assists that night.

A week later in a game at the Pond against Winnipeg, Don had a chance to play against goalie Bob Essensa, his old roommate and teammate at Michigan State. Working the point on the power play late in the first period, McSween took a pass from Peter Douris and slapped a shot towards the net. The puck hit a diving Winnipeg defenseman. It dipped in the air and fooled Essensa. Bob couldn't stop the puck. After playing over six years in the minors, Don scored his first NHL goal against his best friend in the league.

After the game, a 3-1 Mighty Duck win, McSween talked about a moment he wasn't sure would ever happen. "I've been getting some shots and I thought, maybe I would get one. It's just a great feeling. Now I can tell my sons about this, and I have the puck to prove it," said McSween.

McSween described how the goal looked to him. "As soon as I went to wind up, their guy was starting to go down. As he went down, it grazed against his shin pad. It put some spin on it. As it came to Essensa, it kind of skipped on him, and he couldn't handle it," McSween said.

Beating Essensa added to the moment. "It means a little extra because Bob's a good friend of mine," Don laughed. "In the scuffle after the goal, I gave him a friendly jab and asked him if he'd sign the puck after the game. I told him I'd even buy him a soda. It was fun, something I'll remember for a long time."

Most NHL players score their first goal before they've had much chance to imagine it. Almost thirty years old, Don had had years to dream. "You think about beating four guys and scoring, but the great players don't even do that," said McSween. "Most of the time, it's goals like that. Getting the puck and putting it on net. That's hockey."

The only regret that Don had was that his family could not see his first NHL goal. "Unfortunately, my wife and kids are down in San Diego. She wasn't able to get in," explained McSween, whose wife and two sons would join him in Anaheim a few days later. "After the game, I just made a quick phone call and she was very happy. She's waited a long time for it, too."

Don was glad he'd continued playing in the minor leagues. "It wasn't easy to persevere, but I've always loved the game. I've always gone to the rink with a smile on my face, happy to be able to make a living just playing a game," Don explained. "My wife's been behind me. That's important when you have a couple of kids. She knew I had a dream to play in the NHL. She always said, if you have that dream, keep playing."

Don wanted to thank all the people who'd made his big moment possible. When you accomplish something you've always wanted, you should remember all the people who guided you. If you hadn't had teachers, coaches, family and friends helping you out along the way, you could never have reached your dream.

Wayne Gretzky is the greatest hockey player that ever lived. He has a huge amount of talent, but he might not have become a superstar if he hadn't had a lot of help. If Wayne's father hadn't watered down the backyard to make a rink for Wayne each winter, Wayne would never have become such a great player. All of us need help sometimes. That's the way it is.

5

THE UNITED NATIONS

How many of the Ducks do you think grew up in California? If you said none, you're right. The Ducks grew up in big cities and little towns in Canada, the United States, Sweden, and Russia. When you read this chapter, you might want to have a map of the world nearby. That way you can see where the Mighty Ducks come from.

The Mighty Ducks speak English, French, Swedish, and Russian. They came together in Anaheim to play hockey. They get along despite their different backgrounds. They were born thousands of miles apart, but now they all wear the Mighty Duck jersey.

Before every NHL game between a Canadian and an American team, two national anthems are played. If they played the national anthems of every

THE MIGHTY DUCKS OF ANAHEIM 43

Stu Grimson agreed with former rival Todd Ewen not to take any foolish penalties.

player on the Ducks, they'd have to play four anthems each night. The United Nations is a place in New York City where all the nations of the world come together to talk to each other. The Ducks dressing room is like a little United Nations.

Patrik Carnback is a good example. Patrik grew up in Sweden which is a Scandinavian country next to Finland and Norway. When Patrik became good enough, he joined a team in the Swedish professional league. He played for that team for six years before coming to North America to play for the Montreal Canadiens. Now he's a Mighty Duck.

When he joined the Ducks, he often centered a line with Stu Grimson and Todd Ewen, the team's two enforcers. Patrik wanted to show the team his offensive abilities, but sometimes this was hard playing with Todd and Stu. He would get frustrated, because he'd always been a good scorer and playmaker in the past, but he kept working hard to show the team what he could do. Finally, after a lot of other players got hurt, Patrik had a chance to show his stuff. He played his best hockey of the season, scoring goals and setting up linemates.

If you went into the Duck locker room and hollered, "Where's Patrik?" the other players wouldn't respond. You see, everyone calls Patrik "Carns." Nicknames are a great way for friends to show affection, and are very popular among hockey players. A few of the Duck nicknames are: Ron Tugnutt is "Tugger." Bob Corkum is "Corky." Tim Sweeney is "Sweens." Steven King is "Rusty" on account of his red hair. Randy Ladouceur is "Laddie."

Almost every player from Europe gets a nickname because the North American players and coaches often find it hard to correctly pronounce their name. The players from Europe included the Swede, Patrik Carnback (Carns), and the Russians, Alexei Kasatonov (Kasa) and Anatoli Semenov (Tony). It's easier to get somebody's attention by calling out a short name during the game, anyway. Try it yourself. Which is easier: "hey, Tony" or "hey, Anatoli?"

Not too many years ago, there were no Russian players in the NHL. The government in the Soviet Union wouldn't let their players play in North America. They wanted the best players to stay home. Other Europeans, mostly Swedes and Finns, were free to play in the NHL, but most of them chose to stay at home as well.

A lot of Europeans started to play in the NHL about ten years ago. You might know Jarri Kurri, who is from Finland. A few years ago, one of the best small players in the NHL was Mats Naslund. He was a star in Montreal who came from Sweden. The best goalie in the NHL last year was probably Dominik Hasek (pronounced "hah-shik"), who won

CHRIS RELKE

Rookie Patrik Carnback, the Mighty Ducks's only Swede, learned to play with his teammates and improved as the season went on.

the Vezina Trophy. He's from the Czech Republic.

Most of the best young European players in the world are now in the NHL. The Soviet government collapsed and now Russians and Latvians are free to play here. Two Latvians, Arturs Irbe and Sandis Ozolinsh, and two Russians, Igor Larionov and Sergei Makarov, led the San Jose Sharks into the playoffs last year.

Last year, the league's top goal-scorer and top playoff scorer was Vancouver's Pavel Bure, a young Russian. Pavel is great. Perhaps even better was his friend and former linemate in Russia, Sergei Fedorov. Fedorov led Detroit to a great season and won the MVP award. At the beginning of last season, the Mighty Ducks had two Russian players who were a little older than Bure and Fedorov.

Tony and Kasa, the Ducks' two Russian players, and their teammates didn't always understand each other. When Kasa turned thirty-four, his teammates wanted to celebrate his birthday. Instead of having a party, they decided to play a joke on Kasa.

They bought a whipped cream pie. Two of the players took the pie and snuck up behind Kasa and hit him in the face with it. They wanted to make Kasa feel like one of the boys. No one had done anything like this to Kasa before. His previous teammates in Russia had been all business. He thought the other Ducks were trying to make fun of him. Kasa was mad. Luckily, Tony was able to explain the situation to Kasa. If Tony hadn't been there, Kasa may have stayed angry.

The Europeans came to the NHL from across the Atlantic Ocean. The North Americans came from all across the continent. The Americans came from New Jersey, Minnesota, Massachusetts and New York. The Canadians came from Ontario, Saskatchewan, Quebec, British Columbia, and Alberta.

All the players had one common language: Hockey. Slapshots. Faceoffs. Blind passes. Pad saves. Goals. Shutouts. Wins. Everyone understood these phrases. Whether it was an American, a Canadian or a Russian guarding the Mighty Duck net, he had only one thought in his head—stop that puck.

The Ducks could work together on offense, too. In a game against Dallas in November, Tony Semenov centered a line with Peter Douris on his right and Garry Valk on his left. The linemates who grew up speaking different languages thousands of miles apart ended the night with three goals and seven assists. The Ducks beat the Stars, 5 - 4.

Their ten points proved that players who came from different lands could work together. Todd Ewen and Stu Grimson, the team's enforcers, had fought each other before they joined the Mighty Ducks. Now that they were teammates, they were good friends. They even made an agreement not to take foolish penalties. That way the Mighty Ducks wouldn't have to kill so many penalties, and would have a better chance to win.

In the end, everyone worked together in hopes of a victory. The players might have come from all over the world, but they agreed on how to play winning Mighty Ducks hockey. They learned to understand each other so they could be a better team. The little United Nations was a big success.

6

THE NEW GUYS

Late in their first season, the Mighty Ducks had a chance to make the playoffs. They needed some fresh bodies if they were going to catch the teams in front of them. The general manager decided to go out and find some new guys to help the Ducks. In a trade, though, you have to give up some of your own players in order to get someone else's players.

In February, the Ducks traded Ron "Tugger" Tugnutt to Montreal to acquire Stephan Lebeau, a talented young center. Before Lebeau arrived, another new player, Mikhail Shtalenkov, was brought in to replace Tugger and to back up Guy Hebert. Mikhail (his teammates call him Mike) grew up in Moscow, learning to play a stand-up style by watch-

THE MIGHTY DUCKS OF ANAHEIM

FRANK PRADO/NIHA HOCKEYTALK MAGAZINE

Paul Kariya, the newest Mighty Duck, excited fans with his speed, vision and great hands.

ing great Soviet goalie Vladislav Tretiak.

Mike spent the first six years of his career playing for a team in his hometown. When the Soviet Union collapsed, he moved to the United States with his wife and young son. Before Tugger was traded, Mike had been playing for the Ducks' top farm team, the San Diego Gulls.

He played well in his first three games for Anaheim, but the Ducks only scored two goals and lost all the games. Finally, in his fourth game, he won for the first time in the NHL, nearly shutting out Ottawa.

"I'm just happy today because it's my first NHL win. A shutout would have been great, but it's not very important. If we win, it's more important," Mike said after beating the Senators. "I was surprised when they traded Ron. I thought I'd spend the rest of the year in San Diego."

Another new guy who was surprised to be in Anaheim was Stephan Lebeau. In the summer of '93, he'd been celebrating a Stanley Cup victory with his teammates on the Montreal Canadiens. Unlike Mike, Stephan came to Anaheim alone. He'd grown up in Montreal. When he reached the NHL, he bought his own house and then bought a house for his parents just down the block. Now he was three thousand miles away.

"I grew up in Montreal. I was lucky enough to

play in my city. It was great to win a Cup for Montreal," Lebeau said right after the trade. "Of course, leaving my family was hard, but that's the way hockey is. Next year, I will get a satellite dish for my family so they can watch me play."

Lebeau saw the chance to play for the Mighty Ducks as an opportunity to get to play more. He wasn't angry, just a little sad. "I was happy in Montreal, but it's time for me to turn the page. I have no hard feelings against the organization. I was expecting the trade because my ice time was reduced," Lebeau said. "The pressure is really tough in Montreal. Maybe I'm going to have a normal life here."

Even his loneliness didn't last long. His teammates took him out for a round of golf right after his first practice. He was happy, playing golf in late February when the streets back in Montreal would still be covered with snow. He could see that he was going to fit right in with his new friends. The only problem Lebeau and the Ducks might have would be finding good enough linemates for their young sharpshooter to play with.

Another problem for the Ducks was beating the other teams in California. When they played the Los Angeles Kings and the San Jose Sharks, the Ducks didn't seem all that mighty. In early March, the Ducks finally beat the Kings for the first time.

The effort of new Duck John Lilley (48) impressed teammates Garry Valk (18), Tim Sweeney (8) and Coach Wilson.

Lebeau, who scored two goals, and another new player, John Lilley, made a big difference. Like Lebeau, Lilley was small and tough. In his first NHL game, Lilley gave his new teammates a lift. "He really fired up our bench tonight," said Coach Wilson. "I liked what I saw. He's got a future with us."

Lilley joined the Ducks just after playing for the United States in the Olympics. He was only twenty-one years old, and he'd already realized his dream. "It was a good experience for me to go out there tonight and just work hard," Lilley said afterwards. "There wasn't as much pressure as at the Olympics, but I'd prepared for that all year. Here I just jumped in so I think I was a little more nervous. Your first NHL game is something you've been waiting for your whole life."

After a few games, everybody realized that Lilley was making a difference. He wasn't the strongest player or the fastest, but he was the freshest. John never quit skating at top speed. His style impressed the team's general manager. "He's the kind of guy that, if you're playing against him, you'd just like to stick him." said Jack Ferreira. "When he's on your team, you just love to have him with you."

Despite being outweighed by everyone on the ice, Lilley checked any player he could reach.

"Lilley's a little freight train," said Peter Douris, his teammate. "When he hits you, it's a blow to your ego." Even his coach singled him out for praise. "He doesn't care how much bigger the other guy is," said Ron Wilson. "He plays like he's got a chip on his shoulder. He's right in everyone's face."

Lilley gave his best effort, and so did all the other Ducks, in the final games. And the Ducks played well, winning more games than they lost. Unfortunately, it wasn't good enough. The San Jose Sharks were even better, and the Ducks would have to watch the playoffs on TV, like every other fan.

With their chance to make the playoffs over, the Ducks started to think about next season. They would need even more new players if they were going to get better. The most important new player would be Paul Kariya. Kariya had been the best college player in the U.S. as a freshman at the University of Maine. After his first year at college, Kariya joined the Canadian Olympic Team and led the Canadians to a silver medal.

After the Olympics, Paul left school and began contract negotiations with the Ducks. For the first time he could remember, he was no longer playing hockey in March. Even during his off time, Paul kept working to improve himself.

"I work out six days a week: three days a week skating for two hours a day and three days a week of aerobic conditioning and weights," Paul explained. Being a great left-handed shot didn't satisfy him. "I'm actually trying to work on my right-handed shot and become ambidextrous like Gordie Howe was. It's sort of like starting the game from scratch again. I've got a pretty good one-time shot right now. I'm just working on my stickhandling."

Although he really wanted to be in the NHL, Kariya was happy to be back home in Vancouver. "Everything happens for a reason. It's nice for a change to get to play some street hockey with my brothers. It's been a nice break from a hectic couple of years."

Paul even got to be a fan again, watching Wayne Gretzky, his favorite player, break the all-time scoring record. "I was sitting at home with my family watching the game. It was just a great feeling that I had for him. I got chills down my spine. I've always been a big Gretzky fan, and it was nice to see him get the final record."

Writers and scouts compare Kariya to Gretzky. While it will be extremely difficult for anyone to be as good as Gretzky, what Paul shares with the Great One is tremendous hockey sense and an unyielding drive to improve. "The key thing is to continue improving my strength. I see myself as a playmaker and my overall vision is my strength. I know from seeing the NHL players I have to get stronger."

By the end of the summer, the Ducks had signed Kariya. In Kariya, the Ducks had a top forward on the way, but they were still looking for a top young defenseman. Hockey teams send out their best scouts to find talent. Scouts compare players to other players they've known. Every year, David McNab, the Ducks' top scout, watches hundreds of games all over the world.

Of the dozens of players he talked to last season, one just blew him away: Oleg Tverdovsky, a lanky Russian defenseman. Oleg had grown up in Donetsk, a big mining city in the Ukraine. Oleg left his family behind in Donetsk when he was fifteen to play hockey in Moscow. For two years, he'd lived in a bad neighborhood in an unheated apartment so he could learn how to be a better player. As a sixteen-year-old, he was playing in the top league in Russia.

When McNab talked to Oleg, he was reminded of Buffalo superstar Pat LaFontaine, another player McNab had liked. "Oleg was funny, personable, and relaxed," said McNab. "I knew that was the guy. He would have no problem fitting into the locker room."

No matter where he is on the planet, from Tokyo to Toronto, McNab eats at McDonalds. It's how the other scouts find him. McNab's dinner with Tverdovsky was in a hotel restaurant, but McNab promised to take Oleg to the McDonalds in Moscow the next time he was in town.

At the draft in Hartford, the Mighty Ducks selected Oleg with their first pick, second pick overall. At the team party after the draft ended, Oleg came up to McNab and asked him in perfect English, "Do you want to go get a Big Mac?" McNab looked at Oleg, and the Russian teenager smiled at him. The Russian was already making jokes in English. He would be just fine.

After the Ducks brought in Oleg, they made trades to get two more defensemen, Tom Kurvers and Robert Dirk. The team had lost three of their original defensemen: Alexei Kasatonov, Sean Hill, and Bill Houlder, but there were young faces on the horizon besides Oleg: Scott Chartier, an American, and Nikolai Tsulygin, a Russian.

Along with Kariya up front, the Ducks would have the skilled young Russian wing Valeri Karpov on the team for the first time. No one could wait for the new season. With the new guys joining the players already on the team, the Mighty Ducks would have an even better chance to make the playoffs. One thought passed through the Ducks' minds all summer: let's drop the puck!

MIGHTY STATS
FACTS ABOUT THE DUCKS' FIRST SEASON

Teams that have not beaten the Ducks:
    Winnipeg Jets
    Hartford Whalers
    Philadephia Flyers
    New York Rangers

Teams that the Ducks have not beaten:
    San Jose Sharks
    Detroit Red Wings
    Boston Bruins
    Buffalo Sabres
    Montreal Canadiens
    Pittsburgh Penguins
    Florida Panthers
    New Jersey Devils
    Washington Capitals

THE MIGHTY DUCKS OF ANAHEIM

Biggest Duck: Stu Grimson, at 6'5", 225 pounds.
Smallest Duck: John Lilley at 5'9", 170 pounds.

Oldest Duck: Randy Ladouceur at 34 years old.
Youngest Duck: John Lilley at 22 years old.
(Paul Kariya, 19 years old, and Oleg Tverdovsky, 18 years old, will both play for the 1994-95 team.)

Fastest Duck: Joe Sacco
Slowest Duck: Guy Hebert

Most penalized Duck: Todd Ewen—272 penalty minutes
Least penalized Duck: Bob Corkum—18 penalty minutes

Most goals as a Duck: Bob Corkum, 23 goals
Most career goals: Stephan Lebeau, 110 goals

Most points: Terry Yake, 52 points
Best Plus/Minus: Bobby Dollas, plus 20

Most valuable Ducks: Guy Hebert, Bobby Dollas, Bob Corkum
Most underrated Duck: Garry Valk
Most improved Duck: David Williams

If you liked this book, you might want to read a more in-depth book on the Mighty Ducks, also by Dean Chadwin, called *Rocking the Pond: The First Season of the Mighty Ducks of Anaheim*. You can purchase this book through your local bookstore, or by writing to:

Polestar Press Ltd.
1011 Commercial Drive, 2nd Floor
Vancouver, British Columbia
Canada   V5L 3X1

Ask for a complete list of our more than 20 hockey titles.